Live Out Loud

A Woman's Guide to Kicking Fear, Anxiety, and Self-Doubt in the Face!

Kellene Diana Sampson

ISBN: 978-06924654000
Book Consultant:
Shalena D.I.V.A. Broaster

Cover Photography: Lisa Fleet photography

Cover Design by:
Theresa Campbell

Dear God,

Where do I begin? Boy oh boy. God, if I had 10,000 tongues I couldn't praise and thank you enough! As I write this letter the tears are just flowing. God, I never thought in a million years that all the life tests that you gave me would be my testimony to help millions. Thank you for equipping me with the tools I needed to overcome each and every one of them. I know you aren't done with me yet, but I can truly say that I know now more than ever that I am ready! God I thank you for your grace and your mercy. Even when I didn't believe in myself you still trusted me with the most fragile and precious things along my path. I thank you for revealing to me that my gifts and talents not only will help others, but will continue to help me. God, I ask that you continue to bless me and I promise I will continue to be responsible with my purpose. I love you more than ever God because now I love me! Thank you and I love you soooooooooooo much!

Love,

Your Favorite

☙ v ❧

Acknowledgements

To Jalyn Spears, my beautiful daughter: You are the best thing that has ever happened to me. I thank God for trusting me to take care of such a special, gifted and talented little girl. You are my reason to win in life. Thank you for your resilience and all of your encouraging words. You are my star, my light, and my reflection. I promise I will continue to make you proud to follow my footsteps. There will be bumps in the road just like it was for me, but I promise that you are strong enough to leap over any obstacle and land upon your greatness just like I did. I believe in you and I love you with my whole heart.

To my mother: Ms. Linda Paul. Thank you for being there for me. I know without a doubt you want in every way to see me succeed and Ma, I promise you I will. Just like Jayln, you are my reason to win in life. I feel so honored to have such a beautiful mother that is in my corner and who has always cheered me on. Thank you for your constant reminders that I have the favor of God. I know now more than ever what that means. Thank you, I love you.

To my brother: Mr. Michael Sampson Jr. I don't even know where to begin. You may not know this, but you are truly my rock. Literally in my darkest hour you told me, "Kelle, you are fine." Mikie, I finally believe that! Thank you so much for holding my hand and lifting me up when I was putting myself in an early grave. I thank you for your patience and for your strength. I love you from the bottom of my heart.

To Grandma: Ms. Elaine Paul. Thank you for your prayers. Grandma, I am finally where you prayed for me to be and for that I am forever grateful! I love you more than words can express! I am honored to be a part of a family that you built with love. Thank you Grandma. Love, "Doogie."

To my Coach and Mentor: Ms. Shalena D.I.V.A. and Ms. Sherica Matthews. I thank God every day for you both. I know that God truly worked through the both of you to reveal to me not only my greatness, but my purpose. God is truly amazing and I thank you both for being obedient to him and allowing yourself to be a vessel in helping me achieve my dreams. I love you both from the bottom of my heart! Thank You!

To the father of my daughter: Mr. Jamar Spears. I appreciate your kind spirit and thank you for always believing in me. I will always love and cherish you for giving me the best gift in the world. Our ladybug. Thank you!

To my Father: Mr. Michael Sampson Sr. I love you and thank you for giving me life! I wouldn't be where I am without you. I miss you, but I know you're looking down proud with tears of joy in your eyes! I thank you from the bottom of my heart for the lessons you have taught me before and even after you left this earth. For that, I will forever be grateful. This is just the beginning Daddy, you have a lot to look forward to. In your honor I will succeed.

To Grandma Shirley: Grandma, I love you and I thank you for leaving such a beautiful legacy behind. I miss you, but I know you are restored with wings. You and Daddy are celebrating my success. I love you Grandma Shirley!

To My Stepdad: Mr. June Ellerbe. Thank you for everything. I love you from the bottom of my heart. You have always believed in me even when I was a little girl. Thank you for always allowing me to confide in you and for that I am truly grateful!

To Uncle "Yumpy": Mr. Walter Paul. I love you and I know that God has got you and you are looking down smiling saying, "Go head Doogie." I miss you Uncle Yumpy and thank you for the many lessons of overcoming that you have taught me and many others. For that I am truly grateful. I love you!

To my circle of support: Nakita Paul-Long, Timothy Sheppard, Mia Crawford, Quanique Lundy, Angelique Redmond, John Lambert, Jerrod Simpson, Michael Beard, Ryan Byers, Patrick Fortson, Tangela, Diana Freeland, Towanda Bryant, Letrise Cooke, Shaun Clarke, Pat Clarke, Patricia Norris, Carol Muhammed, Marc Murphy, Alvertino Isaacs, Dr. Marankino, Leslee Gold, Patsy Milner, Carolyn McWilliams, Minister Mac, Kelley Matthews, Raina Logan, Marwan Morgan "Quay" and everyone else who has supported me along my journey I love you all. Thank you from the bottom of my heart!

Dear Gal,

Thank you for purchasing *"Live Out Loud."* There are so many heart-filled lessons for you in the pages ahead but here is a quick list of things that you can expect to take away from reading *"Live Out Loud"*:

In this book you will learn how to:

➤ **Grow** into the person you are destined to be by applying 3 necessary tips

➤ Face the mirror and become comfortable with your reflection

➤ Believe and **ACHIEVE** your dreams

➤ **LIVE** life fearlessly and to your fullest potential

➤ Learn the power of giving and getting **SUPPORT** along your journey

I wrote "Live Out Loud" for you, but it is truly a story of my own journey of overcoming years of fear, low self-esteem and doubt. I actually titled this book *"Live Out Loud"* because for a very long time I was alive but I was not living! I was stuck in my own "What If" way of thinking which caused me to live in fear 24/7! My world looked like a foggy cloud much like that wave of fog you see when you look past a cooking grill. When I finally made a conscious decision to get better I promised myself that not only would I live to make up for all the time I lost due to my mental handicap I decided *to "Live OUTLOUD"*. What that means to me is to live life to the fullest by any means necessary and to give life 150%, achieve my biggest, wildest dreams, and to commit to always looking for ways to better myself so that I can help others do the same. Living OUT Loud allows me to feel free from all the mental chains and shackles that held me captive for years!

Along my journey, I've realized that what I was missing the most was the very foundation I needed in order to live the life I always wanted and deserved. That foundation is Self-Love. For years I have loved on so many people including my daughter, boyfriends, and even my friends but at the end of the day when they are sleep or unavailable I was left all alone with a feeling of emptiness. As long as I was focused on, caught up in others I didn't have time to focus or deal with my own issues. Looking back, I know now that I was hiding the real me in others. For a very long time my happiness and my well-being depended on other people. When they were gone I was left with nothing but the mirror, in which was such a scary place for me.

I was my own worst critic. I thought I was never good enough and I always found fault with myself: my nose was too big, I was too short, my teeth weren't straight enough, my hair wasn't long enough and the list goes on. I was constantly worried about how others perceived me that I did everything for everyone else. I was so unhappy that I started manifesting emotional illnesses like Anxiety and Depression.

It wasn't until I hit rock bottom mentally that I knew I had to take action to save myself—the woman God created to achieve greatness! I made myself a personal promise and commitment to strengthen where I'm weak and to embrace, accept and acknowledge where I'm strong. I had to learn how not to only love myself but how to love myself properly.

Although it has taken some time, Today, I can truly say I enjoy the mirror and I love myself inside and out. I am really glad that I made the CHOICE to get better and use self-love as my healing source. I used to think I would never see the light at the end of the tunnel with all the panic attacks, depression, and self-confusion I had going on. However, I'm here to tell you that once you make a CHOICE to survive any obstacle is possible to overcome even self-doubt and self-sabotage.

I know it is my divine assignment to help as many women as I can to feel this way about themselves too-starting with YOU! Self-Love is hard work but just like anything you need and want in life you have to work hard for it. YOU are worth it.

I wrote this book to share those life lessons with you in a very fun and unique way using my G.A.L.S. philosophy so you, too, can use the foundation of Self-Love as a healing source just like I did.

You should note that the principals I present in this book have worked in my life and the lives of my private coaching clients. I would love to work with you as a client but if I never get that opportunity, I offer this book as a way for you to benefit from these simple yet life changing lessons.

At the end of each chapter there is a "Mirror Check." After you read a chapter I want you to self-reflect and apply the principals you learned in that chapter by doing the exercise and activities given at the end of that chapter.

Always remember that self-love is INNER WORK! It has nothing to do with how long your hair is; what designer bag you wear; or how HIGH YOUR HEELS ARE.

Let the outside be a reflection of you on the inside. Not the other way around.

Be sure to connect with me at the following places:

www.kellenediana.com
https://www.facebook.com/KelleneDiana
https://instagram.com/kellenediana/

https://twitter.com/KelleneDiana

Love Ya!

KelleneDiana

P.S. I hope you enjoy the poem I wrote especially for you on the following page.

Who Am I Without Heels?

by

KelleneDiana

Who am I without HEELS?
I'll tell you who
I am a woman who stands TALL with or without
High Heel Shoes

Who am I without HEELS?
I'll tell you who
I Am a BOSS, that knows she is worthy of success
Just like you

Who am I without HEELS?
I'll tell you who
I am a woman with substance
Building her own EMPIRE too

Who am I without HEELS?
I'll tell you who
I am a woman who laughs at the stereotype
That Sweats and SNEAKS can't be fabulous too

Who am I without HEELS?
I'll tell you who
I am a Leader with goals and dreams
To be made Anew

Who am I without HEELS?
I'll tell you who
I am a Mother who teaches her daughter
That it's what inside that count
And what will make her true

Who am I without HEELS?
I'll tell you who
I am a woman who struts confidently
In her purpose
Just like God said I would do

Who am I without HEELS?
I'll tell you who
I Am KelleneDiana

Table of Contents

Section One:

Grow

CHAPTER 1

Love Yourself First

"To soar in life you must first learn to F.L.Y.
(first love yourself)."

~Mark Sterling

Successfully moving forward in life requires you to first accept and acknowledge that we all have room for improvement no matter what stage in life we find ourselves. It's inevitable that as people we will grow naturally, but we have to make a conscious decision to grow with direction and purpose. When you make the decision to take control of the direction you are headed in life you must first look for the biggest, brightest mirror you can find and start with self-reflection. You have to be willing to strip down naked to a vulnerable state and be completely honest with yourself. Sometimes the mirror can be a scary place, but it's the only place where healing and growth can begin.

Although there are many ways to grow, there are three key ways that turned my life around. First you MUST love yourself. Loving yourself is one of the most important things you can do. Many times, we focus on loving others so much that we neglect ourselves. As women, we are natural caregivers. So it comes naturally for us to love and care for our children, our husbands, our parents, the homeless, the sick and shut-in. We constantly give and give, but when we get home and look in the mirror, we criticize ourselves and tear ourselves down. We pass judgment on ourselves for the extra five pounds we put on, for the mistake we made in our lives five years ago. We even pass judgment on ourselves for things that are out of our control.

Love does not tear down. Love is gentle. Love is kind. Love is patient. How often are you gentle with yourself? How often do you speak kind words to yourself and about yourself? When was the last time you encouraged yourself? Why is loving yourself so important? You teach others how to treat you by how you treat yourself. Self-love is important because there will be times when you will have no one but yourself. And when that happens, you have to know how to love yourself out of any situation. Otherwise, you will find yourself stuck and feeling hopeless.

"Love yourself first and everything else falls into place."

~Lucille Ball

There have been so many twists and turns on my journey of self-love. Growing up, I was chubby, my nose was fuller than most, my face was fat, I was short and my butt was oddly disproportioned. I remember my older cousins and my friends used to tease me and call me names like Miss Piggy, K-Solo, Ugly, Fat, and the list goes on and on. Even though it was in fun to them it had a huge impact on how I viewed myself. I started seeing the things they called me looking back at me in the mirror, which in turn caused me to be very self-conscious and lack self-esteem. I used to say to myself "I wish I looked like her, I wouldn't get teased so much," or "I wish I was her, maybe he would like me." It had gotten so bad I stopped smiling because when I smiled my nose would spread and look even bigger. The mirror became harder and harder for me to look into.

As I got older and loss my baby fat, my face got slimmer, I grew into my nose and I felt better about myself. However, I wasn't yet to the point where I was in love with who I saw in the mirror. Just when I was getting to a point of acceptance I remember I went to a neurologist because I was having horrible migraine headaches. During my visit I discovered that I have a very unique asymmetrical face. Yes, one side is different than the other. The doctor told me it's not harmful, just unusual. After that I was battling with that mirror all over again. I couldn't take pictures looking straight ahead. I couldn't look people in the face without thinking to myself *they are looking at all my imperfections.* I was self-conscious all over AGAIN. I just wanted to hide.

At this point I was getting on my own nerves. I thought to myself there has to be a fix, that's when I learned and understood the power of The Serenity Prayer:

> *"God grant me the serenity to accept the things I cannot change; courage to change the things I can, and wisdom to know the difference."*

That same mirror that I was so afraid to look into became a healing place. I learned the meaning of stripping down naked and being honest with who is staring back at me. No makeup, no fake hair, no lip gloss. I went toe-to-toe with Kellene Sampson. What I discovered is that the unusual asymmetry in my face, my full nose, my full lips, my big round bottom, the way my breast lay, my short legs, my size 7 ½ feet is what makes me so unique, and my uniqueness is what is most beautiful! I finally thought to myself *how other people view me has no bearing upon how I view myself. How I view myself is all that matters and what counts.* The things that I could change I did. I wasn't happy with my weight; I had control over that so I joined a gym. I set fitness goals, I changed my diet, and before I knew it I lost thirty-one pounds. I wasn't happy with the clothes I wore, so I went shopping and I purchased things that made me feel and look good

---

"If you feel BEAUTIFUL on the inside it will show effortlessly on the OUTSIDE."

~Kellene Diana

Soon I focused on the things about me that are not of the physical. In that same mirror I reminded myself that although I'm loving my physical self, there is so much more to me than what you can see. I reminded myself that I'm a giving person, I'm now a forgiving person, I am a considerate person, a loyal friend, a great mother, a kind person, a motivator, a helper, and a creator of great things. I realized I had so many beautiful qualities that lay right inside of me. At that moment I became lovable and even more attractive to myself.

I realized that all along, the love and acceptance I was looking for from others would never matter if I didn't love and accept myself. I fell in love with myself. I treated myself with much more respect and I made others respect me as well. I stopped accepting mediocre relationships and started holding myself to a higher standard. I constantly reminded myself that if I didn't love and respect myself, then I couldn't expect anyone else to love and respect me. True love and happiness comes from within. Take the time to explore you; you will be surprised to find all the treasures you have buried that no one else possesses but you!

Mirror Check

What things about yourself do you want to change that is within your control? What steps can you take to make this change?

_____

_____

_____

_____

_____

_____

_____

_____

_____

_____

_____

_____

_____

_____

_____

CHAPTER 2

Forgive

"Anger makes you smaller while forgiveness forces you to grow beyond what you are."

~Cherie-Carter Scott

In order to continue to grow you have to learn how to not only forgive yourself but to also forgive others. Are you holding on to anger, hurt, or pain that was caused by you or someone else? If so, it's time to release those emotions so that you can heal. So you ask how in the world do I do that? The way to identify if you are holding on to pain that was caused by someone else is to monitor and pay attention to how you feel when someone mentions that person's name that has hurt you.

- Does your heart start beating fast?
- Does your mood or attitude change?
- Do you cry?
- Do you still journal or talk about this person?

But what if the person that has hurt and disappointed you is YOU? When you think of things that you have done in the past that you aren't proud of, how do you feel:

- Angry?
- Sad?
- Undeserving of your blessings or favor?

If you answered yes to any of these identifiers then that means you are still holding on to pain, and it also means that you haven't fully forgiven yourself or others. Identification is a major factor in healing, so kudos to you for taking the first step. For a very long time I thought If I were to forgive someone who has hurt me then that would mean I was weak and that I was saying that what they did to me was okay.

I have learned that holding in all these negative emotions towards yourself or the people that have:

- hurt you
- broke your heart,
- stole from you
- cheated you
- talked about you
- raped you
- left you
- abandoned you
- beat you

are detrimental. As painful as those things are, holding on will subconsciously create an emotional illness that will turn your heart cold and cause you more harm and more pain than you know.

I have been heartbroken and disappointed by the ones that have meant the most to me in my life. I had a daddy who chose a homosexual lifestyle that took him away from me at the age of eleven. Right after he died, I was told by my family he died of a heart attack, but found out years later he died of AIDS due to his chosen lifestyle. For years, I was so hurt that my daddy didn't take an extra thirty seconds to protect himself to make sure he would be here for me and my brother. I thought to myself, "Why would he do this to me? We were so close. Didn't he know I would need him in my life? Didn't he know that my brother would need a male figure in his life? Didn't he know how hurt I would be to see him lying motionless in a casket with no breath left in his body?"

There were so many nights when the only thing that would play in my head was: "Why, daddy? It was your choice!"

For so long, I couldn't even embrace the name he gave me. The thought of him made me cringe, cry, shout, get angry, embarrassed, and the list goes on and on. I started talking to a counselor about how badly my dad hurt me, and that was really the first time I learned the power of expression. It felt so good to release all of the deep-rooted issues I had with my dad. I learned how to refocus and remember the great things about my dad, how carefree he was, how much fun he was, how great of a dancer and swimmer he was. All those things brought me joy and made me look at my dad in a positive light and focus on the good things about him. It also made me feel better about myself. I began to have peaceful sleep, I started smiling more and I felt peace. Most importantly, I began to make better decisions for myself.

"Forgiveness is the attribute of the strong."

~Manhatma Gandhi

After I released the pain by journaling and communicating my feelings (good, bad or indifferent), I decided to love myself enough to forgive. As I mentioned, holding on to past pain hurts

YOU more than anything or anyone could ever do to you. I learned and experienced that FORGIVENESS is for your own healing and is one of the best gifts you can give to yourself. Forgiveness is truly a HUGE step in order for you to GROW closer to your purpose in life, which is much greater than the hurt and pain you ever endured in your past. It is so important to understand that the same forgiveness you give to others you need to give to yourself. Always start with healing you first.

Mirror Check

Do you believe that forgiveness will bring you peace? How does forgiveness give you freedom? Explain.

_____

_____

_____

_____

_____

_____

_____

_____

_____

_____

_____

_____

_____

_____

CHAPTER 3

Express Yourself

"Expression is my therapy."

~KelleneDiana

Rappers Salt and Pepa said it best: "You know life, it's all about expression, you only live once and you're not coming back, so express yourself." That was one of my favorite songs growing up because I always had a desire to express myself, but I didn't know how. I was very shy. I was always worried about what people would say or think about me if I really said or did the things I truly desired.

Did you know that suppressing even the simplest thought, emotion, desire, curiosity, and even question can impact your well-being significantly in a negative way? To this day, it's still challenging for me to speak about my feelings directly, so I created my own way. The reality is expression doesn't always mean you have to talk or speak. I learned that there are so many beautiful forms of expression.

"Beauty without expression is boring."

~Ralph Waldo Emerson

I discovered that I'm an awesome poet. I've written poetry about everything under the sun, my mental state, heartbreaks, motherhood, love, sex, etc. At the end of every poem my signature would be "Expression is My Therapy," and it was! I learned that although my poems were rarely shared with others, this was still a great way to express my feelings. I didn't worry about being judged, so my poetry was able to flow and capture my emotions.

I loved writing, but I still had those days where I didn't feel like writing, and I still didn't quite want to talk about how I was feeling. I decided to show how I was feeling through my style of fashion. I started purchasing different jewelry pieces that would speak to me, and I thought in turn if it speaks to me, it would also speak to others. This form of expression was not only effective, it was fun.

When I was feeling bold and confident, I would wear a huge statement necklace with unique shapes and sizes. When I was feeling quiet and shy, I would wear very conservative, simple pieces. When I was feeling like being outspoken, I would wear bright colorful earrings or bracelets. This became another outlet of expression. It made such an impact in my life that I wanted to share the idea with others, women in particular.

In 2009 I got my wholesale distributor's license and created a jewelry line that would capture different moods, versatility, personas, and most of all expressions. My first company, Kellene Diana Statement Jewelry, was born to give women the perfect outlet to express themselves in a distinctive way through unique jewelry collections: Bold & Confident, Quiet & Shy, Loud & Outspoken, and Peace and Freedom. I branded my business with ZEBRA stripes because ZEBRAS represent uniqueness, as no two zebras are alike. I also used the beautiful color sapphire. This beautiful blue hue represents divine power, mental peace, wealth and happiness.

Kellene Diana Statement Jewelry was created to give others the green light to express who they are and what they are feeling even if it is NOT what society is used to. Expression through fashion is also therapy, and I encourage you to embrace your uniqueness, your thoughts, your feelings, and release them for your own healing, sanity and wellbeing. Not only is expression good for you but it's also a way to ensure that others will hear, see or feel your story. Most times when you speak up, whether that be through speaking, writing, or another form of expression, it's a great chance that you will help someone else.

Just like I did I want you to take some time to find an artistic form of expression.

There are so many options you can choose from.

Express yourself by:

- Dancing
- Singing
- Writing Poetry
- Writing Songs

Paint how you feel, you may create a MASTERPIECE.

"It's not just about the art, it's about giving your soul a voice for freedom of expression"

~Desiree East

Mirror Check

Do you ever feel like you know what you want to say in your mind but you don't know how to say it or it doesn't come out right? If so, list three topics that you notice you freeze up about when it comes up. Write beside each topic what is it about those things that causes you to freeze up.

Next, choose a topic and use the guide below to help you express what you are trying to convey

Use this format as a guide...

When I saw/heard_____ I felt_____
because_____ and now _____ so that_____.

_____

_____

_____

_____

_____

_____

_____

_____

_____

Section Reflection

What are 3 ways to grow mentally, spiritually and emotionally? How can you apply these things to your life on a daily basis?

_____

_____

_____

_____

_____

_____

_____

_____

_____

_____

_____

_____

_____

_____

Section 2:
Achieve

CHAPTER 4

Dream. Believe.

"Dreams come a size too big so we can grow into them."

~Josie Bissett

Having a sense of achievement is so important in the G.A.L.S. philosophy because it is a component in validating your self-worth. Achievement takes your confidence and self-esteem to a whole new level and it's something that noone can ever take from you. It is one thing to dream, but to actually achieve something is a huge accomplishment. The feeling that you get when you know that you believed in yourself enough to push through and turn your dream into a reality is a feeling that is very rewarding.

Did you know that people who allow themselves to dream big are usually the ones whose dreams come true? Dreaming big doesn't mean that you are walking around with your head in the clouds, it simply means that you love yourself enough to believe you are worthy of those dreams becoming a reality. Dreaming allows you to reach your destination or purpose while you're on the journey of accomplishing it. Dreams help you to stay motivated by seeing a glimpse of what life will be when you are finally face to face with your potential.

Dreaming is necessary to give you fulfillment even through the obstacles you face that may be set out to discourage and distract you. It is a choice to dream. I encourage you to choose to Dream big and watch your dreams unfold before your very eyes with hard work, passion and dedication, as the more you Dream the more you achieve.

"Logic will get you from A to Z, Imagination will get you everywhere."

~Albert Einstein

I always had a very vivid imagination. As a little girl I used to stand in front of the mirror and sing into my hairbrush thinking I was on stage. I used to say, "One day I want to be a singer, and I'm going to sing in front of millions on stage like Janet Jackson." Although I couldn't carry a tune to save my life, I didn't care because it was my dream. As I got older, my dreams started to reflect the person I was becoming. I started dreaming about many things like being rich, famous, helping others, being on stage delivering a message that will inspire and help others. I dreamt about being a trendsetter and letting people know it's okay to be unique. I dreamt about having a huge fashion show and then coming out at the end to a standing ovation because I am the designer of the jewelry the models were wearing.

These dreams always seemed so far-fetched and out of reach until I learned the POWER of believing in yourself. Remember that old saying? "You can do anything you put your mind to?" Well guess what, that saying is so true! I started channeling the power within me to make my dreams a reality. I had that fashion show on October 21, 2012 and I spoke to eighty-six people from a stage while wearing a beautiful mermaid gown. I wasn't the designer of the jewelry but I was the brains behind creating the collections to represent expressions and coordinating the entire show, which was just as big of an accomplishment.

I remember I could not stop smiling because I was so proud of myself. I finally finished something that I started. As I looked around the room, I realized that the impossible became possible. Every seat was completely filled and with one person standing. I had a sold-out crowd. Something that I never thought I would accomplish. It was almost a very surreal feeling, and I allowed myself to savor the moment and I enjoyed every second of it.

I spoke about the importance of believing in yourself and how important it is to have a healthy outlet. I was very open and honest about my diagnosed panic disorder and depression, and how selling jewelry and networking with other powerful women became my outlet and helped me to cope with my struggles with mental health. Before I knew it, there wasn't a dry eye in the room. I touched that many people in less than an hour. I thought to myself, *OMG, I am standing in my dream*, and I stood tall and strong. After all the years of planning and failing I never stopped believing in my dream or my strength to accomplish it. The stumbling blocks are necessary to strengthen you so when you are standing in your dream and in your purpose you will be ready. Always remember; if you can BELIEVE you can ACHIEVE.

Mirror Check

Imagine yourself standing in your dream. How would you feel?
Be descriptive. Why is fulfilling your dream important to you?
How would it change your life?

_____

_____

_____

_____

_____

_____

_____

_____

_____

_____

_____

_____

_____

_____

CHAPTER 5

Plan. Execute.

"A goal without a plan is just a wish."

~Antoine de Saint-Exupery

Living a life of spontaneity can be fun, however, sometimes it is wise to slow down and think things through to ensure you are setting yourself up to achieve success. Webster defines a Plan as a detailed proposal for doing or achieving something. Once you set your goal or mission it is essential that you not only plan but to plan properly.

After several failed attempts at having a successful business I wondered what I was doing wrong. The passion was there, the connections were there, the merchandise and customers were all there. So why was I still failing? I discovered I was missing the main ingredient to success: Execution with a Proper Plan. I am such a spontaneous person that planning things was always a bit challenging for me.

I quickly learned that to be successful in anything you do in life you must PLAN strategically then execute, not the other way around. I launched my jewelry business December 5, 2009. I obtained my wholesale license, I established tons of distributor relationships, I purchased jewelry, I got the venue, I sent out invitations and I had a great turnout. Although I planned, I didn't plan properly. I didn't have any follow-up and I didn't know how to manage my capital. I didn't have backup inventory, so people were actually fighting over jewelry. Everything looked good on the outside, but if they only knew the chaos behind at the time was "Kelle's Statement Jewelry" they would have left as quickly as they arrived.

Although it was a great turnout and everything looked nice, there was no strategic PLAN in place, so I failed quickly. I kept wondering how all the planning I did months before this event could fail. It seemed like no matter how many times I hit the reset button, I still had the same result: failure. I felt like my business was a failure and worse, that I was a failure. I was discouraged, frustrated and just tired of the cycle. I realized at that point I needed some assistance.

I have such a creative mind and I'm full of ideas, but if I can't plan correctly none of that would matter. I learned the meaning and POWER of networking and asking for help. It is okay to not know it all. God blesses each and every one of us with a special talent that only we can master. Although you should get better at your shortcomings, it's okay to reach out and ask for guidance when needed. Today I am no longer a failure. I am no longer discouraged, and I am no longer doing things on my own. I sought help from business consultants and coaches. Now I have the right team of people around me to help me be successful.

"Closed mouths don't get fed. Today I'm fat, happy and full."

Mirror Check

Name three ways that planning strategically will help you.

_____

_____

_____

_____

_____

_____

_____

_____

_____

_____

_____

_____

_____

_____

_____

CHAPTER 6

Persistence Pays

"Ambition is the path to success, Persistence is the vehicle you arrive in."

~William Eardley IV

How many times have you allowed yourself to dream big, established a proper plan for success, invested time and money only to fail or to be told "no, I'm not interested, or "No, you're not ready" by potential clients or even employers? Times like these it is so easy to get discouraged or even feel like throwing in the towel or giving up. I'm sure we have all been there, I know I have.

It was 2001. There was a buzz about new job opportunities in Owings Mills, Maryland. The word was that if you got the job not only would you get paid very well but you would be able to build your own vehicle that would include full coverage insurance and maintenance. Not to mention health benefits would be free. I thought to myself *wow, I would love to work there and build my car or truck and make all that money.* At that time it was a distant dream because they were only hiring for a collections position. The rumor was, it was impossible to get in there, but to me that was motivation to try. I applied, and although I didn't have much collections experience I filled out the application anyway. I didn't get a call, just a letter saying they went with someone more qualified. I was disappointed but I wasn't discouraged. I continued to do my research about this popular company and found out that I could reapply after six months.

A few months went by and I heard one of my family members got a job there. I went to him and asked him how can I get in? He told me to reapply, so I did. Same thing, got another letter saying they went with someone more qualified. Then before I knew it it seemed like everyone was getting a job there except me! I knew I didn't have collections experience, but I had a good background of reputable employers. What did I do? Six months went by and I applied again. This time I got an actual phone interview, passed that and got a face-to-face interview. I was ecstatic! I just knew I had it in the bag. I was well prepared and I looked depart only to get rejected again.

I was disappointed but I didn't give up pursuit of getting a job.

I took a break from applying for that particular company and I started applying to many other jobs and landed a position at a very reputable investment firm in Owings Mills, Maryland as well. I started there and my career took off. I did such a great job that I got promoted to a Senior Trainer in my department. My pay wasn't the best, but I was content. One day I was at my desk and my cell phone rings, I look down at the phone and it was an unfamiliar number so I didn't answer. I checked my voicemail, and who was it but the HR department of the previous job that I wanted so much, requesting that I meet with them to discuss a Customer Service Position.

I thought to myself just when I didn't apply they found me in their database from all the other times I applied and noticed I had years of customer service experience. I was super excited that I had a chance to sell myself again and this time I had the 5+ years of customer service experience to back me up.

> *"Never give up on something you really want.*
> *It's difficult to wait, but worse to regret."*
>
> *~Author Unknown*

When I went in for my interview surprisingly I was not nervous at all, I walked in there and I claimed it with my confidence. My interviewer mentioned to me she saw how many times I had applied previously and she commended me for not giving up. I shook her hand, thanked her for her time and I hoped for the best. Not even a week later, I got a call, and on the other end of the phone was my Offer of employment. When I tell you I screamed, cried and literally jumped up and down. I was so happy! I thanked the recruiter over and over again. She ran down the pay and all the benefits I previously knew about from all my years of research. I immediately accepted the offer with no hesitation. I gave my two weeks to my current employer, and I prepared for my exit and I couldn't wait until Dec 1, 2008 to embark on my new journey with my new company.

My first day came and not only did I meet people who are still some of my best friends to this day, but as time went on I learned and mastered my job, which put me in a position five years later to be qualified for a higher-paying job as an Insurance Processor. This was in the same field, just from a different angle. I started working at very reputable Insurance Company and there I obtained my Insurance Adjuster license for several states across the country. It was a huge stepping stone that positioned me to be qualified for my job now. I'm currently a liability investigator for another very reputable Insurance company making more than I'd ever imagined. The first time I applied for the first company, I never thought in a million years that it would be my platform to be a successful Wealthy Insurance Liability Investigator for a major insurance firm.

If you have that gut feeling that you're supposed to be somewhere or doing a certain thing, chances are your gut is right. Follow that feeling until the end, do what it takes, approach it at different angles until you are content with the outcome.

"Persevere: to persist in anything undertaken; maintain a purpose in spite of difficulty, obstacles or discouragement; continue steadfastly."

~Author Unknown

With persistence and perseverance is the only way to succeed in anything you do in life. If I had not been persistence in my pursuit of a job, I would not have the dream job that I have today. Just like me, you will encounter difficulties, rejections, and setbacks. These are only temporary. They only become permanent if you choose to accept them as permanent. Instead, get up. Fight back. Persevere. Persist. Keep Going. Continue.

Mirror Check

Name three things that you have given up on that you could have given more time and energy towards. Describe how being PERSISTENT would have helped you accomplish those goals.

_____

_____

_____

_____

_____

_____

_____

_____

_____

_____

_____

_____

Section Reflection

Based on what you have read in this section, Name three ways that how having a sense of Achievement can help you mentally, spiritually and emotionally. Name one activity that you can do daily that will help you to Achieve your dreams and goals.

_____

_____

_____

_____

_____

_____

_____

_____

_____

_____

_____

_____

_____

The Face of Anxiety

By KelleneDiana

The face of anxiety

That's who I've become

The face of anxiety

Sometimes I just wanna run

The face of anxiety

Does anybody know my real name?

The face of anxiety

Learning that I'm the only one to blame

The face of anxiety

Never thought I'd be

The face of anxiety

If only I can be free

The face of anxiety

I hate looking in the mirror

The face of anxiety

The reflection always makes me tear up

The face of anxiety

Will I ever be Kellene?

The face of anxiety

If only I could tuck it away to reach my dreams

The face of anxiety

Wears no makeup
The face of anxiety
Who am I to trust?
The face of anxiety
I hate all the stares
The face of anxiety
Does anybody even care?
The face of anxiety
I'm going to overcome
The face of anxiety
As I am the only one
that can do this for me
The face of anxiety will no longer be
KELLENE
PRAYERFULLY
"EXPRESSION IS MY THERAPY"

Section 3:
Live Out Loud

CHAPTER 7

Fearless

"One who is Fearful will remain distant from their purpose."

~Kellene Diana

Do you want to LIVE or do you just want to exist? You are amazing. You are dynamic. And the world in which you live is just as amazing and dynamic as you are. But in order to live life OUT LOUD and to your fullest potential, you must be healthy, fearless, and you must pause in pursuit of any journey and Take a Breather! This will allow you to continue to be unstoppable and live a life on purpose.

We all have fears, but we all also have choices. When you make the choice to LIVE you then have to choose to LIVE FEAR-LESSLY. Once you remove FEAR and replace it with FAITH the sky is the limit and there is nothing in this world you can't do.

This wasn't always a walk in the park for me. Actually, this was a HUGE struggle for me my whole life. It wasn't until I chose to learn how to love myself properly that I learned the difference between being Alive and LIVING. It takes practice just like anything else you want to master. I took it a step further and I discovered how I can not only live but how to LIVE OUT LOUD and do it FEARLESSLY. Once you focus and establish your worth you will move through life much easier and with purpose. When you have a purpose you learn to push through any obstacle, struggle, and even fear because what's on the other side of that obstacle is much greater.

Like I mentioned previously, I have always been so fearful. Fearful of the unknown, fear of disease, fear of failure, fear of competition, etc. I became handicapped by my fears. I was paralyzed in my own negative "what if" way of thinking. My fearful spirit not only hurt my emotional well-being, but it then manifested and my body responded with multiple panic attacks. I was in a constant state of fear which kept my body in a "fight or flight" state. I worried about EVERYTHING. I remember at one point in time I had been to thirteen medical specialists in less than three months. Every ache and pain I felt I would assume that it was the beginning of something deadly. My mind would get so stuck on that possibility that I would adopt whatever symptoms that were associated with what my mind said was wrong.

Not only was this detrimental to me but also to the people around me. I would call my friends and family, especially my brother, at all hours of the night with a different illness that I had claimed. It had gotten so bad that my friends and family thought it would be best for me to get professional help. I wasn't eating, sleeping, going to work, just twenty-four hours of fear. Not only would an ache or pain trigger these fears, but also movies, commercials, other people's diagnoses and problems as well. I was living in a bubble, trapped in a fear created by my own thoughts. Movies would have such an influence on me that if I considered watching a movie my brother would pre-screen it for me to ensure that it wouldn't negatively impact my spirit and send me in a whirl of fear and panic.

My doctor reassured me multiple times that I was okay. He said something to me one day that was so profound. He said, "Kellene, if you are always worried about dying, when do you have time to live?" He said, "You're young, you're healthy, you have a healthy daughter." He said, "Focus on those things." At that moment a light went off and I realized if I continued down this road I would never LIVE. I would never fulfill my purpose in life.

"Being fearless doesn't mean you have no fears. It means you're strong enough to face them.

~Taylor Swift

I realized that just as much as I tell myself something is wrong I have to tell myself that "I'm okay, I'm healthy, I'm strong, I'm not sick, I'm okay, I'm healthy, I'm strong, I'm not sick," over and over. Just like I force the negative thoughts in my head I realized I had the power to replace them and force positive thoughts. My psychologist said it best, he said, "Kellene, you are very creative, you speak about diseases and possible scenarios I've never heard of, so you are extremely creative." He said, "Now just imagine if you think of something positive, let your mind wonder and create and see how far it will go and create something great!" He told me "Don't use it to hurt you, use that creative ability to serve you."

In that moment I learned that fears are manufactured by you, and guess what, it can also be destroyed by you too. Life is a precious, most beautiful gift from the most high, don't let fears hold you back from living it OUT LOUD and fearlessly just like you deserve.

Mirror Check

Take some time and create a mantra to help your mind and spirit get used to replacing the negative with positive reinforcement.

Example: "I'm okay, I'm healthy, I'm strong, I'm not sick, I'm okay, I'm healthy, I'm strong, I'm not sick."

Every time you start feeling fearful start reciting your mantra.

_____

_____

_____

_____

_____

_____

_____

_____

_____

_____

_____

_____

CHAPTER 8

Get Healthy

"Your happiness is a reflection of your health"

~Healthjunk

Being healthy is a way of life. It's not always about how you look on the outside; it's about how you FEEL on the inside. Did you know that when you work out your body naturally produces a chemical called serotonin? Serotonin is the chemical in the body that calms you and keeps you happy. When you lack serotonin you are more prone to develop mental health issues, so it is very important to stay active in order to stay healthy both mentally and physically.

There is a huge misconception in our society that being healthy means to get on a fad get-skinny-quick crash diet for a quick fix. I've learned in my own experience that this method is very counterproductive. Most times once that crash diet is over you tend to binge and indulge in unhealthy foods and pack the pounds right back on.

Getting and staying healthy is essential in living life OUT LOUD because you physically can't live life to the fullest if you are not feeling good. The great news is, just like with anything else in order to see significant changes in your life you have to make a conscious decision to take the necessary steps to see those changes happen in your life just like I did.

It's no walk in the park, but once you CHOOSE to survive, overcoming any obstacle is possible.

> *"Take care of your body. It's the only place you have to live."*
>
> *~Jim Rohn*

It was a Saturday and I had just gone through a devastating break-up with a man that I loved with my whole heart. Just like most of us do when we are heartbroken, I started eating and drinking to soothe the pain. I went on a day trip with the ladies the next day and I ate and drank some more. That day I had crabs, several beers, chocolate, cake, and fried chicken. Although my body didn't like it I was feeling better emotionally, so I continued to eat poorly. A few days after that I decided to take a fitness class to shed some of the pounds I packed on over that eventful weekend. After the class I looked down at my ankles and they were so swollen. I went home, propped my legs up, changed my shoes and they still didn't go down. I began to worry, so I decided to go to a emergency care facility in my area to get checked out. The ER doctor told me that by my evaluation my salt intake was too high and I needed to watch my diet and lose weight.

He told me this time it's a simple fix; next time it could be a heart attack or diabetes. That following Monday I walked into the office of the Gym manager at my job. I had been crying because I was still upset about my breakup and nervous about what damage I was doing to my body. I sat down and said "I don't know where to start, all I know is I'm 4'11, 196 pounds, my ankles are swollen, my diet is poor and on top of that I'm going through a breakup so I'm depressed." She told me that if I'd commit to coming at least once a day not only would I feel and look better but I would also lessen all those possible health issues I feared so much. With her motivation and my determination my life and priorities literally changed overnight.

I joined weight watchers; I worked out for thirty-five minutes every day on my lunch break. Days I couldn't make it to the gym I would throw in a workout DVD and work out at home. I set goals and I worked hard to achieve them. There were times when the cravings were so great it would bring me to tears, but every time I had a weak moment I would play back in my mind what that doctor said to me. As time went on it got easier and easier, and before I knew it not only was I feeling good but I had lost thirty-one pounds.

It's not only about what you feed your body but what you feed your mind and spirit as well. It is important to treat your body with love and respect so your body will treat you kind in return. There are many ways to do that.

1. Choose the best food for your fuel (organic, fruits, veggies)
2. Meditate
3. Get to know your body and what it rejects
4. Exercise at least thirty minutes daily
5. Stretch.
6. Get a yearly physical
7. Establish a relationship with a primary care doctor
8. Positive Self-talk

"The secret of getting ahead is getting started"

~Agatha Christie

It is important to set small goals and work toward them. If you don't master it on the first few tries don't get discouraged. Keep pushing through because remember, practice makes perfect. Getting, being and staying healthy is a lifelong journey. Along the way you will start to think clearer, your anxiety will decrease, you will become stronger mentally and physically and most of all you will be HEALTHY. Embrace it with all your heart and enjoy the ride. #HEALTHYGIRLSROCK

Mirror Check

Set 1 fitness goal that you can reach in thirty days. Below, write down your 30-day Fitness Goal and how you plan to achieve it.

_____

_____

_____

_____

_____

_____

_____

_____

_____

_____

_____

_____

_____

_____

_____

_____

_____

_____

_____

_____

_____

_____

_____

_____

_____

_____

_____

_____

_____

_____

_____

CHAPTER 9

Take a Breather

"Now and then it's good to pause in our pursuit of happiness."

- Guiliaume Apolliana

In order to avoid a mental, and or physical burnout you HAVE to invest in Self Care. You can do that in so many different ways, but the most important is to simply walk away from your task, close your eyes and breathe. Did you know there are so many wonderful benefits of breathing?

When you simply Breathe you are:

1. Increasing Serotonin and Calming the Mind
2. Centering your thoughts
3. Taking in more needed oxygen
4. Expelling damaging toxins
5. Enhancing your mood

Knowing that an exercise as simple as breathing can bring you peace and serenity is very refreshing in itself.

Although I'm always on a mission to achieve my dreams and goals, I make it a point to "Take a Breather." I absolutely love to dance, so if I'm feeling overwhelmed, I put on some heels, a little makeup, hit the town and I find a dance floor.

One day specifically I was feeling the stressors of my failing relationship, the stress of my 9-5 and the stress of striving to be a successful business owner so much that it brought me to tears. I called my girls and said "I need to get out." I told them to meet me at a local Baltimore Club that of course had a dance floor. I wore a black and gold dress with one sleeve, and the highest heels I could find. I put my braids in a bun and I headed out. I ordered a glass of red wine and ran to the dance floor. I stood in front of the mirror and I let the music take over. In that moment I could literally feel the weight lift from my shoulders.

"If your oxygen mask drops down, it's time to take a breather."

~Richard Simmons

I grabbed one of my girlfriends and we literally danced the whole night away, side by side. Before I knew it, I had stomped out all my stress on that dance floor and the tears stopped rolling. As the night was coming to an end and the music stopped and as I headed out the door I noticed how great I felt. Even one of my girlfriends said "Kelle, I'm so proud of you, I've never seen you so much in the zone like that before." I left all of my stress on that dance floor that night and it felt amazing.

The next morning I woke up feeling renewed, refreshed, and ready to take on the world with a second wind. My thoughts were clear and I was able to refocus. Every successful person has to create a healthy balance, which includes living life OUT LOUD and to the fullest away from work, away from the kids, and away from that title of entrepreneurship. As passionate as we are about those things we still need time to JUST BREATHE.

Mirror Check

Describe how "Taking A Breather" will benefit you. Be detailed. When was the last time you took "A Breather"? What did you do? Did you feel relaxed?

_____

_____

_____

_____

_____

_____

_____

_____

_____

_____

_____

_____

_____

_____

Section Reflection

Name 3 Ways to Live OUT LOUD mentally, spiritually and emotionally. Name at least 1 activity you can do daily that will help you to LIVE LIFE OUT LOUD.

Don't worry about the physical because once you are LIVING Life OUT LOUD mentally, spiritually and emotionally the physical benefits will follow

_____

_____

_____

_____

_____

_____

_____

_____

_____

_____

_____

_____

_____

Section 4: Support

CHAPTER 10

Help Yourself. Seek Help. Help Others.

"You have two hands. One to help yourself, the second to help others."

~Audrey Hepburn

Have you ever consider that if you were meant to go through this life by yourself, you would be the only person who existed on this entire planet? The truth is that we need each other. You need me and I need you. The strongest, most successful people in this world are the ones who are unafraid to ask for help and bold enough to offer help through their gifts. Think of your support system as a part of your foundation—a three-legged chair, if you will. If you neglect one of the three legs, how will the chair stand?

Helping yourself is the MOST important yet most overlooked step that you could ever take in life. So often we put so much work into helping and caring for others that we neglect our own needs. Did you know that we can't do that effectively if we haven't done work to help ourselves first? How many times have you been to a doctor that has been sick? How effective would a teacher be if she first didn't learn? How effective would even a tow truck be if it had a flat tire?

These examples go to show in order to help others you must first be healthy, whole and fully functional yourself. It is important that you acknowledge that we all, no matter what step in life we are in, personally or professional, we can all use a little help.

"Rock bottom became the solid foundation on which I rebuilt my life"

~J.K. Rowling

December 5th 2012 I was evicted from my two-bedroom town home along with my daughter who was five at the time and my six-month-old puppy named Rizen. I couldn't stay with my mom at the time because she had no heat and we were in the middle of winter. It was a struggle going from house to house, sofa to sofa lugging all our clothes, shoes, and our puppy. This was one of the lowest points in my life, and it was even harder because I was unable to care for my daughter the way she deserved to be cared for. I tried to stay strong for her as long as I could, but I eventually slipped into a depression. I couldn't believe this was my life. No job, no car, and now no home. I couldn't wrap my head around that reality. But! Just as fast as I slipped into a depression I quickly came out of it, realizing that although I didn't have the means to provide a home for my ladybug I still had to love and care for her the best way I could.

"The best place to find a helping hand is at the end of your own arm."

~Swedish Proverb

I stopped feeling sorry for myself and I started looking and applying for jobs to put me in a position to be able to get a home on our own again. After I started helping myself by controlling my mindset, keeping a positive outlook and applying myself, I then started seeking and researching help. I found several resources to help single homeless mothers. I applied and was approved for medical assistance for myself and my daughter, and I was eligible for the food assistance program in my community. I was also given several names and number to shelters in my area, which was also a thought-about option as well.

After a few months I was still without a home, but my ladybug and me settled in on my brother's couch. It wasn't the best situation because it was only a small one-bedroom apartment, but he supported my daughter and me the best way he knew how. He made sure we had heat, blankets, TV, water, soap, etc., and we were right down the street from my ladybug's school. I continued to look for work and I continued to keep my eyes open for more resources to help me along the way. I even started going to the gym while my daughter was in school just to keep the healthy chemicals flowing to keep me in good spirits. One morning after my workout I was on my way back to my brother's house to rest until it was time to pick the ladybug up from school and I got a phone call from a job I had applied for months ago.

They were calling me to FINALLY offer me the job. I was so happy, as soon as I hung up with them I screamed at the top of my lungs and the first thing I did was call my brother and tell him the great news. Not only did I get the job, but I would be making more than I was making at the job I'd lost months before. I was so happy and thankful for all the support and resources I had in my darkest hour, but had I not helped myself first I wouldn't have had the motivation to seek help from others. After I started my job I moved in with my mother. I was in a better financial situation and I was able to help her get her heat back on, catch up on bills and I kept food in her refrigerator.

I became her support, and it felt great that I was able to help someone like they helped me. I stayed at my job for a year then I was presented with another opportunity that I mentioned in a previous chapter, making enough money where I no longer need the food or medical assistance program. Now I am in a much better place financially, mentally, and physically. Now not only do my daughter and me live in our own two-bedroom home, but we make it a point to feed the homeless in our community after our dinner outing on Saturdays. Jalyn makes it a point to leave more on her plate to ensure she has enough to give away. We have also helped people financially out of a bad situation to avoid home-lessness and even help prepare food for the homeless. I try to do these things with my little girl as much as possible so she can understand the meaning of not only being support for others but never forgetting that others were support for us.

Mirror Check

Describe a time in your life that you needed help or support from others. How did you help yourself?

_____

_____

_____

_____

_____

_____

_____

_____

_____

_____

_____

_____

_____

_____

_____

_____

_____

_____

_____

_____

_____

_____

_____

_____

_____

_____

_____

_____

_____

_____

_____

CHAPTER 11

Catch a Falling Star

We rise by lifting others."

~Robert Ingersoll

It is a proven fact that one of the best exercises you can do is bending down to lift someone else up! So often we may see someone with all the potential in the world and we cheer them on until we see them fall. But just like anything, if you catch it before it hits the floor it won't break, or most importantly, lose its value.

Ever since my daughter was a small baby she always had a special glow and shine. I knew without a doubt behind those big beautiful eyes was amazing talent and potential. As she got older she proved me right in many ways. First she showed a huge love for music, dancing and singing (gospel in particular). Although she was very young I nourished that talent that she showed and encouraged her to sing and dance until her heart was content. She had a favorite gospel group named RIZEN who is a famous award-winning group that she loved. She learned all the words to their songs, all their dance steps and even knew all their names. If she wasn't watching them in concert on DVD standing in front of the TV doing every dance step to a T she was listening to their CD in the car.

She loved their music so much that she started saying things like "I wish I could meet them." She even prayed for them every night. I thought it would be amazing to show my little girl that dreams do come true if you want something bad enough. So being the creative mom I am, I started researching how I could get in touch with this group. I knew it would be hard, given they are a famous gospel group that travels, but I knew anything is possible for Kellene Sampson, so I put myself to the test. I searched and searched, I found their manger's information and I left several voicemails explaining how their music has touched me and my daughter's heart and has brought us closer to the Lord through their music and how it would be awesome if we could meet them one day.

Months went by, but every so often I would call that number and leave another message. One day I was standing in the break room at my job and my phone rang. It was an out-of-state area code. I was reluctant to answer but I did. When I answered a sweet voice asked could they speak to Kellene Sampson. I said "This is Kellene."

She said, "Hi this is Rizen's Manager and I'm returning your call about your daughter who loves Rizen."

I couldn't believe my ears. My knees buckled and happy tears started rolling. She told me all of my voicemails really touched her and she shared them with the group and they would love to meet Jalyn. I couldn't believe what I was hearing.

Since they tour and live in another state, she said that she could arrange a scheduled call for the group to call Jalyn personally and directly. I was beside myself! We set up a time for three p.m. about a week later. I didn't tell Jalyn because I wanted it to be a surprise. That day came and guess what? At three p.m. sharp they called and they surprised Jalyn with that call.

Jalyn was nervous, but when she was told who was on the other side of that phone, her facial expression was priceless. They talked, they connected, and they encouraged Jalyn to keep on praising the Lord and keep showing her talent through song and dance. After the call I explained to Jalyn how all her dreams are all within her reach no matter how big or small.

Although Jalyn continued to embrace her love for music through song and dance, as she grew a little older I noticed how she started taking an interest in ballet, so I put her in ballet. She completed that. Then I noticed she liked to run, jump, split, and flip. It used to scare me, but I realized this was yet another talent she is showing me, time to pour into this one too. I put her in a local gymnastics program where she learned the basics and how to properly and safely run, jump, split, and flip. There she had a coach who right away saw the great potential Jalyn had to go very far as a gymnast. I took her once a week and I stayed the entire time and watched her and cheered for her on the sideline. We even practiced some of her moves at home to get better. Jalyn quickly went from beginners 1 gymnast to beginners 2 gymnast. Jalyn was sought out and was asked to try out for their competing teams, where she would compete and would have to practice more often. I was all for it.

I took her to tryouts. She tried her best but she was not selected. My ladybug was discouraged and right after her tryouts I held her and told her no matter what, she did great and to pick her head up and be proud of herself. I reminded her that what is for her is for her and nobody can take that from her. Technical results don't change her heart or her passion. We came back and tried again. She continues to get better and better; although she hasn't made the competitive teams she has gained something much more valuable, and that is to keep trying and never give up.

"What you see in others Exists in you."

~Zig Ziglar

Although Jalyn still had a love for gymnastics she started showing interest in basketball, so guess what I did, I put her on a local basketball team with kids her age. I became her biggest cheerleader in this sport just like I did all the others. I cheer her on when she makes a score or set up good defense.

When she loses a game I wipe her tears and remind her of her strength and her resilience. I teach her to embrace losing because she will appreciate when she wins.

By the age of seven Jalyn has been a ballerina, a singer, a gymnast and a girl scout. Although this is a lot for a little girl to some, to me it's important to show our kids at a young age that their dreams are within their reach.

With first the passion and talent they show naturally, then the right support and encouragement from people or a person that wants to see them succeed. Just like the quote says, "If it's in you, you can see it in others when they don't see it in themselves." It's important to be there when they are doing great and even more important to catch them when they should fall so you can place them back where they belong with a lesson to try again until they are content with the results. Just because a star should fall doesn't mean it loses its shine.

Mirror Check

Do you know someone who is struggling in achieving their dreams? Someone that has given up hope on what they want to achieve? If so, call them and point out the talent and potential you see in them that they may have forgotten was there. Tell them how proud you are of them and offer your support.

You can:

1. Share their message on your Facebook page
2. Write them a review on their website
3. Go with them to a speaking event and smile at them from the crowd.

There are so many things you can do, whatever you choose I'm sure your support will mean the world to them.

_____

_____

_____

_____

_____

_____

_____

_____

CHAPTER 12

Never Compete.
Be Inspired.

"A flower does not think of competing with the flower next to it, it just BLOOMS."

~Zen Shin

We each have our own purpose in life. Although the end result or destination can possibly be the same our journey will be different and unique. Our journeys reflect who we are. Embrace your journey, don't compare it to others. Your plan, pain, and process is specifically crafted to strengthen and prepare you and ONLY you for your DIVINE calling and purpose.

When I think of support and competition, one specific friend and scenario comes to mind. She has been my friend for years since I was about eighteen. She was always independent; in fact, I lived with her at one point. In addition to her nine to five, she always had a side hustle. She would sell anything from "off brand" purses to "off brand" cologne and jewelry." I never quite liked any of it, but I still supported her because she was my friend. She was presented with a great opportunity to be a distributor for a "Hot" new garment item that came out. They were very expensive, but I was very excited for her and of course I purchased one. I even joined the movement and became a distributor under her as well.

Although I joined I wasn't passionate about it because I was in the process of launching my jewelry company in December of that year. I shared a lot of information with my "friend" about my distributors where I was purchasing my wholesale jewelry from and I shared a lot of my ideas for my launch with her.

In addition to the popular garment, she was also selling a very popular jewelry brand. My friend used to say to me I should not do my own jewelry thing I should join the company she was working for because it's already structured. Although I thought her advice came from the heart I told her no, I wanted to create my own structure and do my own thing. So with that being said I purchased a whole lot of jewelry to prepare for my extravagant jewelry displays for my upcoming launch.

As my launch date was getting closer I knew I had to start pricing my jewelry for the event to sell and I was absolutely clueless as to what my price points should be so I asked her to help. She agreed so I invited her over to do so. As we are pricing the jewelry, she came up with a great idea to present her garment at my event. I agreed and we were excited about the collaboration. She purchased a few garments to show and sell at the event, I advertised the collaboration on my flyers, she invited people etc. The big day came and about 30 people came for my presentation and a few came to support her as well. My show/presentation was a huge success and I had lines of people prepared to purchase.

Although my friend gave an outstanding presentation she didn't get the sales and interest she anticipated. She was disappointed in the outcome, but I still told her she did a great job. After the show, me and a few close friends and family stayed to celebrate my launch and toast to my success. My friend started packing her things to leave and I went to her and reminded her before she leaves to pay me for the bracelet she was holding during the show to avoid anyone else buying it. The bracelet had a $15.00 tag on it and she said she didn't have change, and then she said "You can't let me go for $15.00"? I said no, I need the money for it or you can leave it and not purchase it. She and I started to argue, I told her she needed to leave because I didn't want to ruin my night or hers. She gave me the bracelet and she left. I didn't hear from this friend for months.

About a month later I went onto her website. Not only was her garment for sale but also some very familiar pieces of jewelry from very familiar distributors were for sale as well, not to mention jewelry for children as well. She was now selling the same type of jewelry I was selling at my launch. I sat on it for a while, but I eventually called her and told her how I felt. I didn't mind her expanding her product base and what her brand offers it was just done very tasteless in my opinion. I was very hurt and I no longer trusted her. She told me she already had it in the works before I launched my business, she just kept it to herself. It took some time, but I eventually got over it. As years went on as my business was failing over and over her business was growing very rapidly.

She went from selling online to local customers to selling internationally she went from that to having her own store in the heart of downtown Baltimore, to selling clothes, shoes, accessories, doing makeup, etc. Then from there she moved into a huge beautiful storefront location in a very prestigious area in Baltimore County reaching all nationalities and she has over 17000 followers on social media and her business continues to grow. Although it took a long time for me to look beyond our "issues" I began to look at her for the role model and successful business owner she was. I will never take the credit for her success.

"When you've worked hard, and done well, and walked through that doorway of opportunity, you do not slam it shut behind you. No, you reach back, and you give other folks the same chances that helped you succeed"

~Michelle Obama

I learned to look at it as Great minds think alike and it's OKAY to share the same ideas with other people. Success is big enough for everyone to get a piece. Not only have I supported every endeavor that she has accomplished I found myself being inspired and motivated to do better in my own business. If she can do it so can I. We have our issues even to this day but I never take what she has taught me for granted. I admire her and my business and dreams will come true because I saw it happen for someone right in front of my eyes with hard work, passion, and dedication. The next time you feel like you're competing with a friend, a mate, a co-worker etc…DON'T COMPETE, BE INSPIRED.

"Complete each other. Don't compete with each other."

~Linda K. Burton

Mirror Check

Do you find that you like to compete? What is it about competing that makes you feel good or bad? How can you turn competition into something positive?

_____

_____

_____

_____

_____

_____

_____

_____

_____

_____

_____

_____

_____

Section Reflection

Name 3 ways that supporting others and getting Support can help you mentally, spiritually, and emotionally. Name 1 activity that you can do daily to remind you that Support others is just as powerful as getting Support.

_____

_____

_____

_____

_____

_____

_____

_____

_____

_____

_____

_____

My beautiful **G.A.L.**,

This may be the end of this book but I am so excited that this is the beginning of some great things for you. Now that you have the tools to **Grow, Achieve, Live Outloud and Support** it's time to put the things you learned into ACTION. Use this book as a guide and refer back to all the lessons as often as you need to.

If you haven't done so already, I encourage you to go back through the book and do all the exercises at the end of each chapter and section. Those exercises played a big part in what helped me to become the women I am today. I am confident they will do the same for you. Also, you can download or purchase the hardcopy of the **G.A.L.S.** Workbook which will keep you busy with additional activities and points to ponder which will further enhance what you have already learned.

I have taught several lessons in this book but always remember to love who God made you to be first. Mind, body, and spirit. Once you master that everything else will follow.

This book was written with pure love and it has been my pleasure inspiring you, encouraging you and pushing you to be the GAL that God wants you to be.

Love You to Pieces!

KelleneDiana

P.S. Remember, if you are beautiful on the inside it will show effortlessly on the outside.

If you are interested in working with me one on one please visit my website at www.kellenediana.com and introduce yourself. Until then stay connected via

www.kellenediana.com

https://www.facebook.com/KelleneDiana?fref=ts

https://instagram.com/kellenediana/

https://twitter.com/KelleneDiana

Upcoming Project:

My memoir is coming soon! Trust me, you don't want to miss it. I'm sharing some of my most painful moments that catapulted me into my destiny. If you could write a letter to your younger self, what would you say? I explored this idea with my upcoming book. I poured my heart out and allowed my words to bleed on the page. I wrote it not to just give an account of my life, because we all have had hardship, but I wrote it to help change lives.

As an added BONUS I've provided a sneak peak! I hope that you enjoy it.

Sneak Peak

Dear, "Kelly"

I remember when you went through losing your father. I know how devastating that was. You were so young. You were 11 and your brother was 12. I know how close you were to him. Ya'll used to have dance contests, you went on his company picnics, the talks on the phone, and I remember he used to show up on Christmas with bags of gifts for you and your brother at your Grandmother's house. Every moment with your dad was so special. I remember all of a sudden he stopped coming around and being the inquisitive person you still are (lol). You asked your mom why you couldn't see your dad. Where is he? Why haven't we talked to him? Your mom told you, he is just a little sick and you will see him when he gets better. You were relieved by what your mom told you and you couldn't' wait for the green light to go see him again. That day never came.

You and your brother came home from school after carrying your heavy Trombone from band class that day only to find your WHOLE family there. Your aunts and your grandmother were in attendance. It was so unusual to see them there during the week because they lived in Baltimore city and you lived in Chase Maryland , which is about a 35-minute drive from Baltimore city. You asked, "why is everyone here?" I remember you and Mikie sat down in the living room with them. You sat on the floor and your brother sat on the arm of the sofa. It got quiet and your mother said, "Kelly, Mikie your father went to heaven this morning."

Kelly, I remember you immediately fell back on the floor so hard, and your brother was sitting there with the blankest stare. He kept saying he was so mad at God. The whole family was there to support you both during this news and I know you were glad they were there because it was an extremely hard pill to swallow.

I could only imagine the pain and confusion you were feeling. It was so hard to see you this way but with time you learned to accept that your dad was gone in the physical, you accepted and trusted that the diagnosis that was given that your dad had a heart attack. Although life was different without him, you managed. You did well, I was super proud of you, you were growing to be a decent young lady, you did well in school, you stayed out of trouble. You started partying a little too much, but you were okay!

You became really curious about life in general. You were 18 and had already been with women and your boyfriend was a local stripper. Gosh, this was hard for me to watch. You were so unsure about who you were becoming. I could see such a beautiful, talented, young lady on the outside with all the potential in the world. You second guessed all of that. You were battling with your current lifestyle and you were ashamed of all the things you had done at such a young age especially being with women.

You were so excited when you learned you could turn to your "Aunt Theresa" and open up to her because she was not as judgmental as the other members in your family. I remember you felt so much better after you expressed to her what you had been battling with. You felt relieved and a huge weight was lifted. You were so happy you had someone you can trust to confide in about your deepest darkest secrets and struggles. You guys started hanging out together more and I remember one day you guys went to the market down the street from your house. As you were walking through the store a song came on the overhead speakers and you told your aunt how much you love the song even though you had no clue who the singer was. Your aunt said, "Wow Kelly your dad loved this song too. Her name is Phoebe Snow and your dad loved all her songs! She said he would smile just like that when he heard one of her songs. You immediately felt so good to know that you shared your dad's taste in music. As you and your aunt continued to shop; going up and down the aisles you were still jamming to the song and reminiscing about your dad. All of a sudden your aunt says, Kelly, music isn't the only thing you have in common with your dad. With a smile on her face she said your dad was also Gay, so maybe you get that from him too so don't feel ashamed about it. You love your dad so now you can love this about you too. You looked at your Aunt with your eyes as wide as the supermarket and asked, "What are you talking about?" You said, "so are you saying my dad was Gay?!" She said yes and then she dropped a BOMB! She said, "and that's why he died, you know your dad died of AIDS because he was gay right?" At this point, you had the biggest lump in your throat and could barely swallow from holding back the tears. You asked, "So he didn't die of a heart attack?" Your aunt assured you that was a lie and he really died of AIDS. On the ride home, there was complete silence because you were in complete and total shock and didn't know what else to say. You pulled up to your house she went in her home and you went in yours. You only lived like 4 doors down from each other. You came in the house and flopped on the sofa still in complete silence.

Tears were just rolling and you called your mother at work and screamed "MOMMY, DID DADDY DIE OF AIDS BECAUSE HE WAS GAY"?!! She said, "I'm on my way" and hung up the phone on you.

I hope that you enjoyed the Sneak Peak! Please stay tuned for the release date of "Dear Kelly!" I can't wait to share my life and experiences with you!

Be sure to connect with me on social media so you can be the first to know when its released

www.kellenediana.com

https://www.facebook.com/KelleneDiana

https://instagram.com/kellenediana

https://twitter.com/KelleneDiana

About the Author

Kellene Diana Sampson is an Author, Inspirational speaker and Self-Development Mentor. She helps women from all walks of life to build a solid foundation of self-love. She believes that in order to Live Life OUTLOUD Fearlessly and to your fullest potential you must first start with a Foundation of Self-Love!

Kellene Diana offers an Empowerment program called G.A.L.S. which is the vehicle she uses to not only help herself but to help her clients achieve all the great things in life they deserve and desire. She also has a member-based network that coincides with the G.A.L.S. program which allows her clients to stay connected to each other for support, ongoing encouragement and account-ability.

Kellene Diana resides in Baltimore, Maryland with her beautiful, loving daughter who is truly her motivation to win in life.

It Doesn't Have to End Here!

Find me on social media. I would love the opportunity to speak with you.

www.kellenediana.com

https://www.facebook.com/KelleneDiana

https://instagram.com/kellenediana

https://twitter.com/KelleneDiana

Luv Ya's,

Kellene Diana